Learn to Move!

I DO GYMNASTICS!

By Bray Jacobson

Gareth Stevens PUBLISHING

Please visit our website, www.garethstevens.com. For a free color catalog of all our high-quality books, call toll free 1-800-542-2595 or fax 1-877-542-2596.

Library of Congress Cataloging-in-Publication Data
Names: Jacobson, Bray, author.
Title: I do gymnastics! / Bray Jacobson.
Description: Buffalo, New York : Gareth Stevens Publishing, [2025] |
Series: Learn to move! | Includes index.
Identifiers: LCCN 2023045848 | ISBN 9781482466072 (library binding) | ISBN 9781482466065 (paperback) | ISBN 9781482466089 (ebook)
Subjects: LCSH: Gymnastics–Juvenile literature.
Classification: LCC GV461.3 .J336 2025 | DDC 796.44–dc23/eng/20231024
LC record available at https://lccn.loc.gov/2023045848

First Edition

Published in 2025 by
Gareth Stevens Publishing
2544 Clinton Street
Buffalo, NY 14224

Editor: Kristen Nelson
Designer: Leslie Taylor

Photo credits: Cover, p. 23 Master1305/Shutterstock.com; p. 5 Sergey Novikov/Shutterstock.com; p. 7 makalex69/Shutterstock.com; pp. 9, 24 (leotard) Michael C. Gray/Shutterstock.com; p. 11 New Africa/Shutterstock.com; p. 13 Dmytro Gilitukha/Shutterstock.com; pp. 15, 24 (balance beam) kali9/iStockphoto.com; pp. 17, 24 (rings) Ilya lyubchenko/Shutterstock.com; p. 19 Peruphotart/Shutterstock.com; p. 21 Undrey/Shutterstock.com.

Printed in the United States of America

CPSIA compliance information: Batch #CS25GS: For further information contact Gareth Stevens, New York, New York at 1-800-542-2595.

Contents

I do gymnastics!
I go to class each week.
My friend Jasmine
goes too!

We dress to move.
I wear shorts.

Lucy wears a leotard.
We do not wear shoes.

First we stretch.
Henry touches his toes.

Bella bends to the side.

It is time for the beam.
Kelly goes first.

Joe hangs from the rings.
He pulls himself up!

Kia likes the bars.
She can do a flip!

We all do handstands.
We use a wall to help.

We get stronger!

Words to Know

beam

leotard

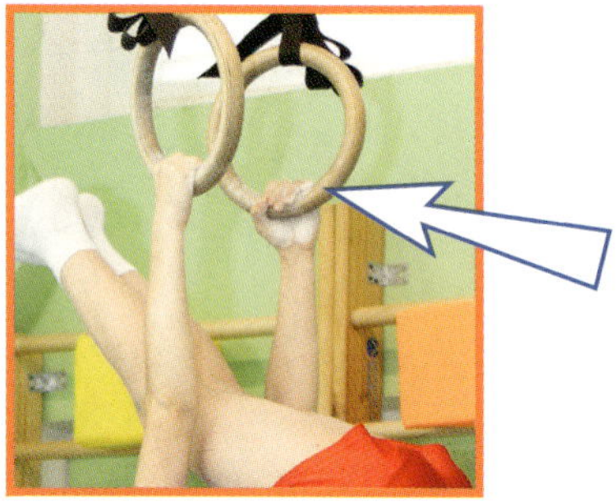

rings

Index